THE LENTEN SEASON

Ash Wednesday

I, II, III, IV, V Sundays of Lent

HOLY WEEK

Palm Sunday

EASTER TRIDUUM

Holy Thursday

Good Friday

Holy Saturday

Easter Vigil

THE EASTER SEASON

Easter Sunday

II, III, IV, V, VI Sundays of Easter

Ascension of the Lord

Pentecost

ORDINARY TIME

SOME SOLEMNITIES IN ORDINARY TIME

Trinity Sunday

Corpus Christi

Christ the King

An Introduction to
the Liturgical Year

Text by Inos Biffi
Illustrations by Franco Vignazia

Gracewing.

Originally published as
Piccola Guida al Messale; L'anno liturgico,
copyright © 1994
Editoriale Jaca Book spa, Milan.

English translation copyright © 1995
by William B. Eerdmans Publishing Co.
255 Jefferson Ave. S.E.,
Grand Rapids, Mich. 49503

This edition published 1995
through special arrangement with Eerdmans
by Gracewing
2 Southern Avenue, Leominster, HR6 0QF, England

Printed in Italy

British Library Cataloguing-in-Publication Data

A catalogue entry for this book
is available from the British Library

ISBN 0 85244 293 9

Imprimatur
in Curia Arch. Mediolani die 21 febbraio 1994
Francesco Coccopalmerio
provicarius generalis

In most instances, Scripture quotations
are from the New American Bible,
© 1986 Confraternity of Christian Doctrine,
Washington, D.C.

Introduction

The events of the life of Jesus are not definitively passed: they live again in the liturgical year. The Church relives them with loving and grateful memory, and appreciatively receives the infinite blessings that come from them. In every Christian celebration the gift of salvation is renewed.

This book was created to help readers understand these feasts as they appear one after another in the missal, and to inspire a desire to participate in them. The illustrations evoke the events of Christ's life, doing so with the incisive and suggestive power of images. The text describes these events briefly, and above all explains their significance.

With the wisdom and further explanation of parents or catechists (who are called to be companions on this wonderful journey through the sacred year), this book can help children begin to feel the attraction of the life of Jesus, and to discover it in the memorials and solemnities of the Church, which mark Christian time and enrich it with grace and beauty. This book will also be helpful to converts.

But readers will not only be instructed in the liturgical calendar and its annual cycle of dates; with persuasive and careful invitation they will be introduced to the celebrations themselves, in which the dates on the calendar are transformed into words, gestures, symbols, and songs; in which faith continuously rediscovers its origins and life regains its vitality.

In this way not even a single hour will be wasted, but all time will be spent in the secure company of Jesus, who leads us from the fleeting days of earth to eternity.

The Liturgical Year: The Time of the Lord

Since the beginning — in other words, since the creation — humanity awaited the coming of Jesus, our Savior. The Virgin Mary gave birth to him in Bethlehem. After having preached the good news, Jesus died on the cross for our salvation. He rose on the third day and poured out the Holy Spirit on the Virgin Mary and the Apostles.

The celebration of these events makes up the liturgical year, or the Time of the Lord.

The Memory of Christ in the Church

The liturgical year is the life of Christ lived out again in liturgical time — in the time and in the memory of his Church. While Sunday recalls the events of Easter, in the course of the year all the mysteries of Christ are relived: from his Birth to the Passion, from his Death to the Resurrection, and from his Ascension to Pentecost. The Saints are also

remembered throughout the liturgical year.

This involves more than simply remembering the facts of Jesus' life. Indeed, in the celebrations of the Church, we relive these events, and they continue to give us grace. For this reason, time doesn't seem like a meaningless passing of years that ends in old age. Instead, time is in the hands of our risen Lord. It is a path that we travel in communion with Christ, who has become an invisible companion of our days as we eagerly await his glorious coming.

With its celebrations, the liturgical calendar marks the stages of this path each year.

Part One

ADVENT AND CHRISTMAS

The first cycle of the sacred year is centered on the birth of the Lord. The event of the Son of God descending from heaven, "for us and for our salvation," could not be forgotten by the Church. Therefore, the Church created a variety of celebra-

tions related to his birth. In addition to Christmas and the Epiphany, there are the days of awaiting them, so that these celebrations do not find us unprepared, with our spirits distracted and empty. The first coming of our Lord still awaits its perfect ending in his second coming.

During this first part of the liturgical year, the eyes and hearts of all Christians are fixed on Jesus, who has once for all entered into time and has illuminated it, filling it with his grace. He draws us continually and fills us with desire.

THE ADVENT SEASON

The liturgical year begins with Advent, which lasts four weeks. During this time, the Church prepares to celebrate the birth on earth of the Son of God, or his first, humble coming among us.

Jesus knocks at the door of our hearts every day, but Advent makes us

particularly attentive to his continuous visits. It helps us remember that "He will come again in the splendor of glory and will call us to enter into his promised kingdom." During the season of Advent, while we wait for Jesus' birth at Christmas, our waiting for the final and definitive coming of Jesus is reawakened and strengthened.

He Will Come to Judge

At the end of the world, in the hour that only the Father knows, Jesus will appear as Judge and glorious Lord.

When we die, we will be judged individually, and we will be rewarded or punished depending on whether we have accepted or refused Jesus' love. But when he comes again, everyone will be judged.

Jesus, who is the only one who can judge, will reveal and reward all the good deeds — even the most secret — of the righteous, and find and condemn those who are wicked. His faithful disciples,

including those who have loved him without ever meeting him, will rise then in a splendor of glory, for a happiness without end. The many who have rejected or betrayed him will be destined to eternal punishment.

During Advent, the Church invites us to think about the Last Judgment with trust, since we will be judged by a merciful Lord, but also to anticipate the final coming of Jesus with proper fear, since he will be a just Judge.

Vigilant Anticipation

We must vigilantly anticipate the coming of the Lord every moment of our lives, since he will come without warning. When we do this, we will resemble the wise young girls in the parable told by Jesus. These girls were well-prepared. They had oil in their lamps when the bridegroom arrived, so they were able to light the lamps in order to be welcomed into the wedding feast. However, the foolish young girls who had no oil for their lamps had to leave to buy oil. When they returned, they were sent away; they were too late to enter the feast.

During the weeks of Advent, we are insistently reminded not to become lazy or negligent in our faith. Instead, we must pray with more passion, be more solicitous in our acts of charity, and be more attentive to Jesus' daily visits to our hearts. Only if he finds us ready will he say to us those most desired and consoling words: "Come, blessed, into the kingdom of my Father" (cf. Matt. 25:34). With good deeds we go to meet the Lord who comes.

The Promised Redeemer

Jesus does not come to the world unawaited. Even before he created the world, God had established that he would give his Son to humankind. He promised him as a Savior after the sin of Adam and Eve. God cursed the serpent, who is the image of the tempting Devil: "I will put enmity between you and the woman, and between your offspring and hers; he will strike your head, while you strike at his heel" (Gen. 3:14-15).

The hope, kindled then in the hearts of humankind, did not go unfulfilled. The "woman" of whom God was speaking is Mary, the Immaculate, whom the Devil has never stained with a drop of sin. Her offspring is Jesus, her Son, who by dying and rising has freed humankind from the slavery of sin and from the penalty of death. This is how the head of the serpent was crushed and the Devil was conquered.

The Tree of Jesse

Jesus comes from the Hebrew race. Among his ancestors we recall: Abraham, the faithful patriarch, who was willing to offer God his son Isaac; Jacob, who wrestled with the angel; Boaz and his wife Ruth, a foreigner from Moab, who was the grandmother of Jesse, the father of King David, the singer of the Psalms; and Solomon, who reigned with wisdom and justice. To these the Evangelists add other branches to Jesus' family tree, finally coming to Joseph, "the husband of Mary. Of her was born Jesus who is called the Messiah" (Matt. 1:16). In addition, Saint Luke traces his roots back to Noah, the builder of the ark, and even further back to Adam, the first human being created by God. From this genealogical tree, formed of sinners as well as saints, came Jesus, the Son of God, who became truly man to save the human race.

Son of David, Son of Abraham

Among the ancestors of Jesus, two stand out in a special way —David and Abraham. Matthew begins the genealogy of our Lord with these words: "the genealogy of Jesus Christ, the son of David, the son of Abraham" (Matt. 1:1).

The angel Gabriel made

this announcement to Mary: "Behold, you will conceive in your womb and bear a son, and you shall name him Jesus. . . . The Lord God will give him the throne of David his father, and he will rule over the house of Jacob forever, and of his kingdom there will be no end" (Luke 1:31-33). Also, the two blind men who asked to be healed called Jesus "Son of David." And when Jesus entered Jerusalem, he was greeted by the sound of "Hosanna to the Son of David!" David was king and singer of God's praises with the Psalms, but the true and eternal majesty is not the fragile one of this world but belongs to Jesus. He will offer to the Father perfect praise.

Jesus is also called "Son of Abraham." The promise of a descendant made to Abraham was fulfilled completely when Jesus, fountain of blessing and universal grace, was born. He affirmed, "Abraham has seen the day of my birth and rejoiced in it" (John 8:56).

Hope in Exile and Tribulation

The people of Israel, from which Jesus came, experienced countless trials. After the slavery in Egypt, the worst of these trials was the deportation to and exile in Babylon. But God did not abandon the exiles. While they cried along the riverbanks of Babylon, he comforted them with the voice of the prophets, and he helped them repent and pray. He kept alive the memory of Jerusalem. He gave them the hope of returning to their land, the restoration of a kingdom, and a new Jerusalem. He also gave them hope for one who would be sent, a Messiah, who would free them. Those exiles did not yet know it, but the true and definitive liberator would be Jesus, sent to save his people.

Foretold by
the Prophets

To revive his people's faith in the coming of our Savior and to prepare their hearts to receive him with dignity, God sent messengers of his word and his promise several times.

During Advent, those voices of comfort and hope ring out in the Church. They help us prepare to celebrate the birth of Jesus with pure souls and keep alive in our hearts the hope for his return as Judge and Lord. The Church will hear again the prophecy of Zephaniah: "Rejoice and exult with all your heart — the Lord is in your midst"; or the one of Habakkuk: "He will surely come and he will not be late"; or of Joel: "Fear not; it will be your salvation"; or of Zechariah: "Your King will come and with him all his saints; he will break the yoke of your slavery"; or of Micah: "Bethlehem: from you shall come forth for me one who is to be ruler in Israel." Nor will it stop Malachi with this alarming message: "The fiery day is coming, and it will make stubble of the arrogant."

But, most importantly, Isaiah's unexpected prediction will be heard: "The Virgin will conceive and give birth to a Son, whom she will call Emmanuel (God with us)." With the prophet the Church will renew the fervent prayer: "Shower, O heavens, from above: let the clouds rain down righteousness; let the earth open and give us the Savior."

Awaited by the Just

"All the patriarchs have acclaimed you," says a liturgical song sung on the day of the Epiphany. "Of you all the prophets have spoken." Along with the patriarchs and the prophets, many others have also felt deep in their souls the need for Jesus. This includes not only the people of Israel but all of humanity from the beginning. All who loved the truth and listened to their conscience (which is always a divine light) discovered a mysterious sense and nurtured a

deep desire that a Savior would come. This started with Adam, once he repented of his sin.

The desire for a Savior was a grace Jesus instilled in human hearts from the beginning. Because of that grace, the desire to do good was born in human beings, and they offered sincere and humble prayers. In fact, human beings have always lifted their prayers to God, even when they hardly knew him.

This is why we say that the just — known only to God — have awaited Jesus and that they have received him. "All the hearts of the just," ends the liturgical song, "have received you."

Zechariah and Elizabeth

Even the angels yearned and waited for Jesus. When it was time for his coming, they placed themselves in the service of God with eager obedience. They prepared for the immediate arrival of his Son into the world.

Vignazia

But Jesus had a forerunner: John the Baptist. The angel Gabriel appeared to Zechariah in the temple, during the evening offering of incense, and said to him, "Do not be afraid, Zechariah, because your prayer has been heard. Your wife Elizabeth will bear you a son, and you shall name him John. And you will have joy and gladness, and many will rejoice at his birth" (Luke 1:13-14).

Zechariah, like Elizabeth, was just and blameless before God, but he doubted Gabriel's words. They came true nevertheless, because they were the words of God. Even though Zechariah and Elizabeth were old and infertile, they did have a son, but until the day he was born, Zechariah was struck mute because of his lack of faith. He did not believe that, with God, all things are possible. In fact, John and especially Jesus are gifts of God; they are amazing and incredible signs of his grace.

Mary and Joseph

The angel Gabriel appeared to Mary of Nazareth, the promised wife of Joseph, with an even more joyous announcement. Greeting her as "full of grace," always and immensely loved by God, he announced that, by the work of the Holy Spirit, she would become a mother. "Behold, you will conceive in your womb and bear a son, and you shall name him Jesus. . . . The Holy Spirit will come upon

Vignazia

you, and the power of the Most High will overshadow you. Therefore the child to be born will be called holy, the Son of God" (Luke 1:31, 35).

Joseph was not the earthly father of Jesus. However, Joseph, along with Mary, was chosen to raise Jesus and educate him in work and in prayer, with watchful and loving care. It is this mission that the angel revealed to Joseph while he slept: "Joseph, son of David, do not be afraid to take Mary your wife into your home. For it is through the Holy Spirit that this child has been conceived in her. She will bear a son and you are to name him Jesus" (Matt. 1:20-21). Mary the Virgin and Joseph, an upright man, believed and obeyed the word of the angel. From the very beginning, they awaited Jesus' birth. They would be the family of Jesus.

The Visitation and John the Baptist

After the angel's announcement, Mary, who carried in her womb the Son of God, Jesus, quickly went to her relative Elizabeth, who was expecting her son, John. Elizabeth pro-

claimed Mary "blessed among women," because Mary believed God's word to her. But the mother of our Lord knew that all this was the pure and unmerited choice of God in his divine grace, who looked upon his servant in her lowliness (Luke 1:48), and she raised to God her most joyous and moving song: the Magnificat.

During Mary's stay at Elizabeth's home, John was born. His father Zechariah gave him the name John, writing the name on a tablet because he was mute; and at that moment he began to speak again. Like Mary, Zechariah sang a joyous song to God, who "has visited and brought redemption to his people" (Luke 1:68). Indeed, God had called that child to become a prophet and the forerunner of the Messiah, Jesus.

In illo tempore:
Exiit edictum a
Caesare Augusto, ut
discriberetur uniuer
orbis. Haec descri
omnes in
Ascendit autem

THE CHRISTMAS SEASON

After the season of Advent comes the Christmas season, which extends from the First Vespers of the Nativity on the evening of the Vigil of Christmas, up to the celebration of the baptism of Jesus. During this time, we celebrate the birth of Christ in Bethlehem, the Holy Family, the Solemnity of Mary, Mother of God, and the visit and adoration of the Magi. We also commemorate the Saints: Stephen, the first martyr; John the Evangelist; the innocent children slaughtered by Herod; and Archbishop Thomas Becket, who was killed in his cathedral. At the end of the Christmas season, we celebrate Jesus' immersion in the waters of the Jordan River.

This is a time of both sorrow and serenity, of distress and joy.

Jesus Is Born in Bethlehem

According to the prophecy of Micah, Jesus was born in Bethlehem, the city of David, where Joseph and Mary had to return for a census. In a poor home that was almost a cave, a manger was the cradle for the child. To announce that the child was the Savior, an angel appeared to the shepherds, who were watching over their flocks at night. Surrounded by heavenly light, he announced "good news of great joy": "Today in the city of David a savior has been born for you who is the Messiah and Lord. And this will be a sign for you: you will find an infant wrapped in swaddling clothes and lying in a manger" (Luke 2:11-12). With that angel, a multitude of the heavenly host began praising God: "Glory to God in the highest, and on earth peace to those on whom his favor rests" (Luke 2:14). Meanwhile, the shepherds hurried to find Mary, Joseph, and Jesus. When they returned to their sheep, their hearts were filled with wonder, and they praised God for all they had heard and seen.

Stephen

During the days of Christmas, some of the Saints gladden the memory of the Church. The first one is the Deacon Stephen, who began a glorious line of martyrs in the Church. Therefore, he is called the Protomartyr. He was stoned because he did not betray Jesus. But even as he was being pelted by the stones, he could see Jesus in the opened heavens, and he prayed to him, forgiving those who killed him.

John

Then comes John the Evangelist. He is portrayed next to an eagle because he, more than the others, gazed with the penetrating eyes of his faith into the mystery of Jesus, the Son of God made man.

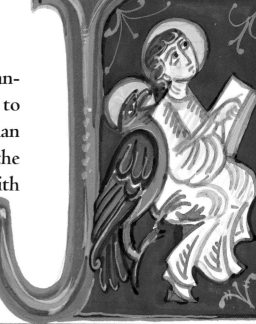

The Holy Innocents

Next follows the Feast of the Holy Innocents. They were the children slaughtered by the jealous and cruel King Herod in his attempt to destroy Jesus, whose kingship he foolishly feared.

Thomas Becket

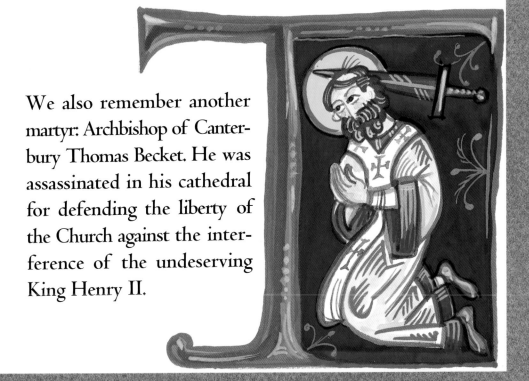

We also remember another martyr: Archbishop of Canterbury Thomas Becket. He was assassinated in his cathedral for defending the liberty of the Church against the interference of the undeserving King Henry II.

Holy Family

Jesus, Mary, and Joseph in Nazareth

During the Christmas season, an entire celebration is dedicated to the Holy Family of Nazareth: a simple family, hard-working, reverent toward God, who above all loved one another. However, even this family faced difficulties: the persecution of Herod, the flight and the exile in Egypt, the dangerous return, and who knows how many other daily problems. However, like every family, they were given the strength to continue by having faith in God.

Jesus was educated by Joseph and Mary. They taught him to pray, to work, to love, to believe, and to be respectful, courageous, and sincere. Therefore, "Jesus advanced [in] wisdom and age and favor before God and man" (Luke 2:52). The Church sees the Holy Family as a "true model," and it asks that "in our families the same virtues and the same love flourish."

The New Year

The Mother of God, the Circumcision, and the Presentation

At the beginning of the year our affectionate memory turns again to the Virgin Mary. On this day we honor her as the "Mother of God," since the Son of God, by the work of the Holy Spirit, became flesh in her, pure as a lily. But this day is also the eighth day after the birth of

Jesus, so we also commemorate his circumcision (by which he joined the holy people of the covenant), and his being given the name Jesus, which means "Savior." Later comes the Feast of the Presentation.

The presentation occurred when Jesus was forty days old. Joseph and Mary carried him to the temple of Jerusalem, to be offered to the Lord. They gave the gift of the poor, two doves, and the righteous Simeon could finally see and hold in his arms the Salvation and the Light of Israel, and prepare to die in peace.

The Manifestation

HERODION

When Jesus was born, a single star rose in the East and announced his birth to the Magi, who came to Jerusalem in search of him. In that city, the "newborn King of the Jews" was ignored by all. But when Herod the King heard of this, and learned from the reading of the prophecy about Jesus' birthplace, Bethlehem, he decided in his heart that he must destroy Jesus, and he ordered a slaughter of children. The Church commemorates this event with the Feast of the Holy Innocents.

When the Magi, guided by the faithful shining star, arrived at the place where Jesus was, they bowed down before him. They offered him gold, frankincense, and myrrh, and then they returned to their country.

The Church commemorates the adoration of the Magi on the Epiphany, or "manifestation" of Jesus. The Magi were representative of all the peoples who would, following them, recognize and adore the Lord.

The Baptism of the Lord

Jesus in the Waters of the Jordan

The liturgy celebrates the memory of Jesus' baptism with great solemnity. John, the prophet sent from God to preach the conversion of hearts in preparation for the coming of the Messiah, received Jesus at the banks of the Jordan River. Of course, since Jesus was not a sinner, he did not have to be purified. Therefore, John at first refused to baptize him. But Jesus wanted this rite performed nonetheless, because it would express his solidarity with the sinners for whom he would die on the cross.

In the life of Jesus, his baptism is very important. In fact, as soon as he came out of the waters, the heavens opened, the Holy Spirit descended on him in the form of a dove, and a voice proclaimed, "This is my beloved Son, with whom I am well pleased" (Matt. 3:17). This is how it was revealed who Jesus is. This event foreshadows Christian baptism, which gives new life through the Spirit and renders human beings sons of God, in likeness to Jesus, who is the Son of God.

After this celebration, Ordinary Time begins and continues until the beginning of Lent.

Part Two

LENT, EASTER, AND THE EASTER SEASON

After the seasons of Advent and Christmas, which center on the birth of Jesus, a new cycle begins, which takes its meaning from Easter. We arrive at Easter after following the penitential days of Lent to their conclusion at the Paschal Triduum of Holy Thursday, Good Friday, and the Easter Vigil. Then we proceed with the Easter season. This is a time of joy, which we spend continuously remembering the resurrection of the Lord, which encompasses all of the events of salvation history.

Pentecost concludes the Easter season with the celebration of the outpouring of the Holy Spirit, the fountain of all the gifts of grace, from which the Church is born.

After the Easter season, the liturgical year continues even in Ordinary Time, following the sequence of various Sundays. But other important celebrations occur during this time. These celebrations include Trinity Sunday, the Feast of Corpus Christi, and finally the Feast of Christ the King, which solemnly concludes the liturgical year.

THE SEASON OF LENT

The Church does not rush to the celebration of Christ's passion. Instead, it makes use of the entire Lenten season, which starts on Ash Wednesday and ends on Holy Thursday with the celebration of the Lord's Last Supper. The ashes are an austere and eloquent symbol of these forty days. They reveal our will to be converted and to do penance when faced with the grace of forgiveness

won and offered by Jesus, who was crucified. The ashes are placed on our foreheads with the words "Turn away from sin and be faithful to the Gospel" or with the admonishment "Remember that you are dust, and to dust you will return."

It is from this dust that Jesus will raise us, making us participants in his glory, if we allow our lives to be renewed through his mercy.

Ancient Periods of Forty Days

In the Old Testament, the number forty occurs frequently, as if it has a mysterious significance. So it is not unusual to encounter events lasting forty days, which serve as both prelude to and prophecy of Jesus'

forty days in the wilderness and the Church's forty days of Lent.

The Flood lasted forty days, and in its waters were buried the corruptions of men and women, so that there could be the beginning of a new life with the righteous Noah. The journey of the Jewish people from Egypt through the desert to the Promised Land lasted forty years. And it took the fiery prophet Elijah forty days, during which he was sustained by bread and water from the angel, to cross the desert in order to meet with God on Mount Horeb.

The "Lent" of Jesus

Today, the Church knows Lent as forty days of prayer and fasting. In this sense, we can say that even Jesus experienced Lent. After his baptism, he spent forty days in prayer and fasting in a deserted place, acquiring the strength to reject the temptations of

Satan, the Devil, who attacked him at the end of the forty days.

Satan tried to discourage Jesus from listening to the Word of God. He tried to lure Jesus away from his future humiliations by tempting him to perform showy miracles and trying to seduce him with the promise of earthly power. First he tempted Jesus to turn the desert stones into bread, which he could easily have done, since he was the Son of God. Next Satan tempted Jesus to perform a miracle by throwing himself from the Temple rooftop so that angels would save him. Finally, Satan tried to seduce him with the promise of power over the earth. However, Jesus dismissed the Devil without the slightest hesitation, giving himself to the mystery of saving the world by dying on the cross.

On our Lenten journey to the cross, our commitment to resist temptation is renewed by the example of Jesus, and we are supported by his grace.

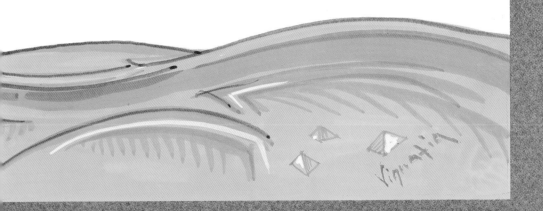

Toward the Cross: The Objection of Peter

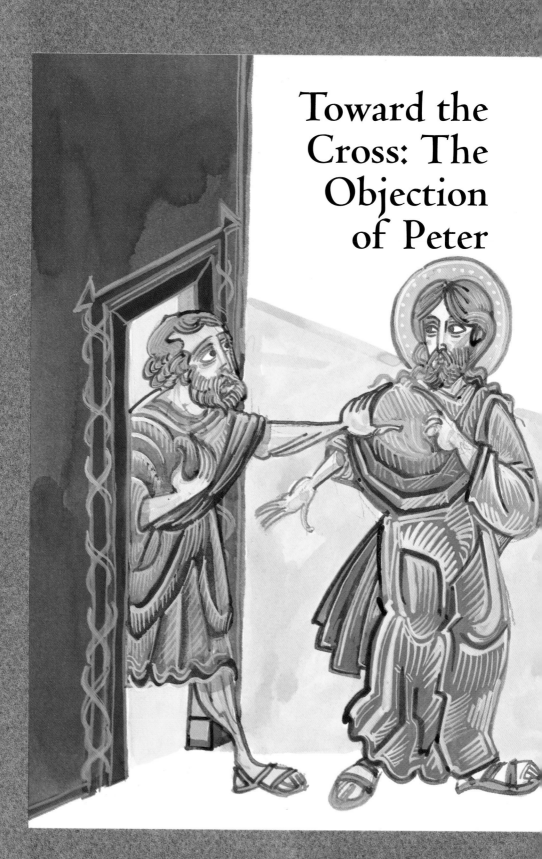

It was completely unheard of and unbearable that Jesus, the Messiah, the Son of God, would die on the cross. In fact, Peter could not accept this. He reacted violently when the Lord announced that in Jerusalem he would have to suffer a great deal, be sentenced to death and crucified, and then rise on the third day. Taking Jesus aside, Peter tried to discourage him, but Jesus responded with a stinging rebuke: "Get behind me, Satan! You are an obstacle to me. You are thinking not as God does, but as human beings do" (Matt. 16:23). Without realizing it, Peter was trying to tempt Jesus exactly as the Devil had done in the desert.

During Lent we recommit ourselves to being true disciples of Jesus, carrying the cross after him. In this way, we become his true friends.

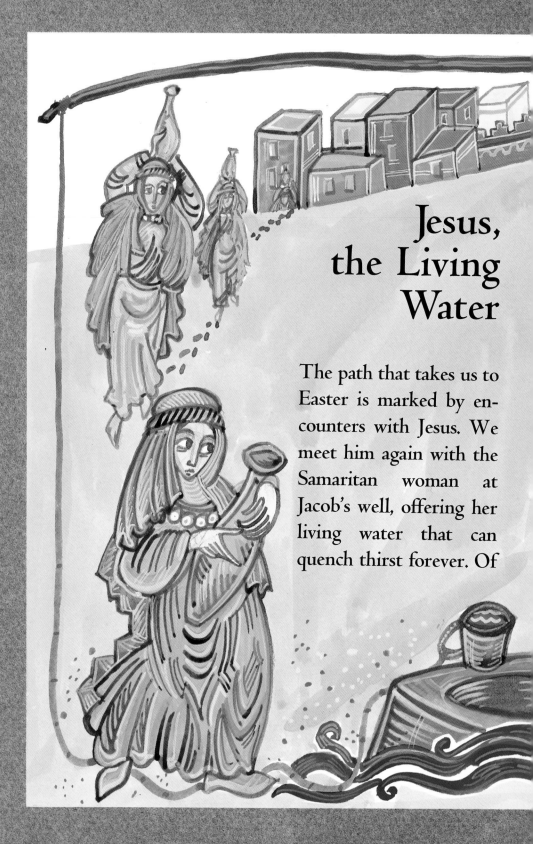

Jesus, the Living Water

The path that takes us to Easter is marked by encounters with Jesus. We meet him again with the Samaritan woman at Jacob's well, offering her living water that can quench thirst forever. Of

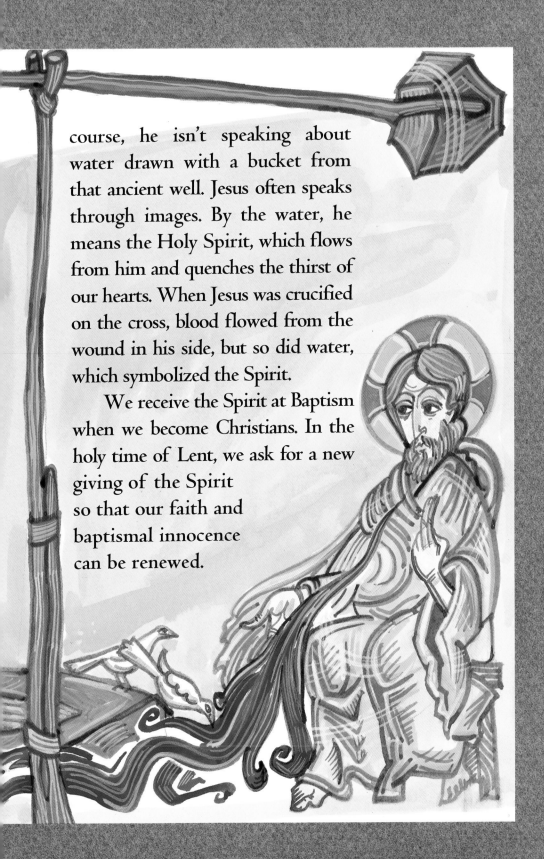

course, he isn't speaking about water drawn with a bucket from that ancient well. Jesus often speaks through images. By the water, he means the Holy Spirit, which flows from him and quenches the thirst of our hearts. When Jesus was crucified on the cross, blood flowed from the wound in his side, but so did water, which symbolized the Spirit.

We receive the Spirit at Baptism when we become Christians. In the holy time of Lent, we ask for a new giving of the Spirit so that our faith and baptismal innocence can be renewed.

"I am the Light of the World"

Jesus is not only the source of living water, which is the Holy Spirit. He is also the light of the world. For the man born blind, Jesus miraculously opened the eyes of his body. But that action was a sign pointing to an even more wonderful miracle — how Jesus gives the light of faith to the eyes of the soul. Baptism is the sacrament of rebirth in the Spirit, and

at the same time it is called the Sacrament of Enlightenment, because the Christian, with faith, sees everything in the light of Jesus, as if with his eyes.

This light should, especially during Lent, shine in the most intimate crevices of our conscience to reveal all hidden sins. This is necessary so that we can confess them with sincere and penitent hearts to the mercy of Christ, which is the most precious and necessary grace that we receive in the Church. Lent is a time of penance and forgiveness.

"I am the Resurrection and the Life"

Easter, which Lent leads us to, celebrates Jesus' victory over death. The miracle of the resurrection of Lazarus is a prelude to this victory. Jesus, source of the Spirit and of Light, is also the Fount of Life — "I am the resurrection and the life," he says; "whoever believes in me, even if he dies, will live" (John 11:25).

To those who have faith, Christ gives the grace of Life, which destroys death from sin and is the pledge of resurrection. We receive this grace in the rebirth of Baptism. However, if we fall into mortal sin and refuse that grace, we are given the grace of life again in the Sacrament of the Reconciliation.

Lent especially is the season for this sacrament, in which are loosed the bonds that keep us slaves of sin, which brings us death.

HOLY WEEK

Palm Sunday

"Hosanna to the Son of David"

Easter is now near. Jesus, humble and peaceful, enters Jerusalem, festively welcomed and acclaimed. This triumph announces what will come later, with the Resurrection. But first, there will be the very sad days of Jesus' passion and death. The blessed palms and olive branches displayed in our homes remind us that these days — the days of

Holy Week — are about to begin. They invite us to dispose our hearts with intense affection to relive these days together with Jesus, who, giving himself to an unjust condemnation, bore the weight of our sins. With his death he washed away our guilt, and with his resurrection he won for us salvation.

Mary of Bethany, the Betrayal of Judas, and Preparing for the Last Supper

After Jesus' entrance into Jerusalem, our memory recalls a sweet figure and a sad figure. The first one is Mary of Bethany, the sister of Lazarus and Martha. As a sign of her complete and freely given love for Jesus, she wiped his feet with costly perfumed oil and then dried them with her hair. The second figure is Judas, a greedy thief, who disapproved of this affectionate gesture. He could not comprehend it be-

cause his self-interest and ambition were what tied
him to the Teacher. In fact, during these days he
arranged to betray Jesus for thirty silver coins.

We relive the precious and solemn days of Holy
Week with the pure and ardent soul of Mary, instead of with the cold, unfeeling soul of Judas.

Holy Thursday

The Last Supper

The Easter Triduum begins with the Mass of the Lord's Supper on Holy Thursday and ends with vespers on Easter Sunday. For the last time Jesus eats the Passover meal with his disciples: the lamb, along with the unleavened bread, the wine, and the bitter herbs. In this way he institutes his supper. As Saint Paul tells us, "The Lord Jesus, on the night he was handed over, took bread, and, after he had given thanks, broke it and said, 'This is my body that is for you. Do this in remembrance of me.' In the same way also the cup, after supper, saying, 'This cup is the new covenant in my blood. Do this, as often as you drink it, in remembrance of me'" (I Cor. 11:23-25).

The Mass renews the Last Supper of the Lord. It is the living presence of his sacrifice and communion with his Body given and his Blood poured out.

Judas takes part in this supper, but Jesus knows that Judas will betray him. He says, "He who has dipped his hand into the dish with me is the one who will betray me" (Matt. 26:23) — and Judas is the one.

Good Friday

The Cross

Good Friday is a day of bitterness and mourning. We are spiritually focused on Christ's cross. The Church altars are stripped of their adornments. Our hearts and all of our thoughts are turned to Jesus crucified, who, abandoned by his friends and with the tender help and presence of his mother Mary — Our Lady of Sorrows — dies on the cross for the salvation of all humankind. His immense love atones for all of their — and all of our — sins. With him, we turn to the Father; in him, we rediscover that we are brothers

and sisters, and we all will embrace in the universal prayer.

Today we will hear the exclamation "This is the wood of the cross on which hung the Savior of the world," and we will be invited to venerate it. By surprising mystery, "From the wood of the cross is come the joy of the whole world."

Jesus was crucified between two criminals. One of them turned to Jesus, trusting that Jesus would remember him, and was able to hear the most comforting words: "Today you will be with me in Paradise" (Luke 23:43).

Holy Saturday

The Burial and the
Descent to the Dead

After Jesus died, his body was taken down from the cross, wrapped in a cloth, and laid in a tomb carved in a rock, in which no one had yet been buried. Holy Saturday is spent in the anxious and silent remembering of Jesus in the stillness of his burial and in his encounter with all the just who have faithfully awaited him. On this day no rite is celebrated. We spend time in church only to pray and meditate near the place where the eucharistic body of Jesus was placed.

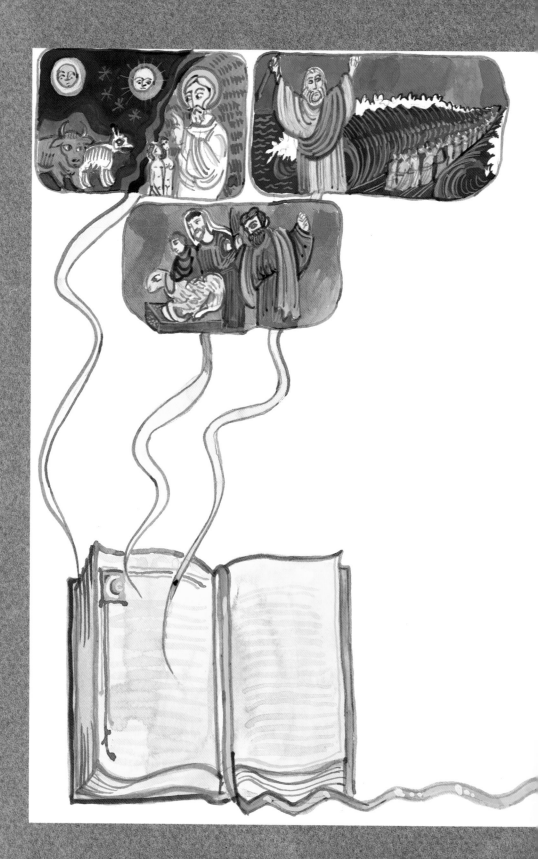

The Easter Vigil

A "Night of Grace"

There is no vigil more solemn or richer in ritual than the Easter Vigil. The new fire is blessed to be a guide "to the feast of eternal splendor." The Paschal Candle is lit as a luminous symbol of Jesus, the "Morning Star which never sets," while there rises to God the song called the "Exsultet." It is well-known and joyous because it calls "happy" even the fault "which gained for us so great a Redeemer."

The sacraments of the Christian initiation are celebrated: Baptism, Confirmation, and the Eucharist. And all of salvation history is re-evoked in the biblical readings about the creation, Abraham and Isaac, the passage through the Red Sea, and other prophetic events which Jesus, risen from the dead, has fulfilled. Now the Resurrection should appear in the truth and purity of our lives.

THE EASTER SEASON

The Appearances

For fifty days, from Easter Sunday to Pentecost, the Church continues to fix its attention and its heart on the risen Jesus and to re-invoke his appearances. These appearances generated and strengthened the

certainty that Jesus' resurrection was not an ingenious fantasy or a pious way of remedying the bitter disappointment of his death.

Even though Jesus no longer belonged to the physical world, nonetheless these people really did see him: Mary Magdalene and the other women; Peter, James, and the other Apostles who ate with him; and a great number of Disciples. From their experience, we are reassured that "the Lord has truly been raised" (Luke 24:34). The victory of Jesus over death is the heart of our faith, which otherwise would be deprived of all its content.

The Supper at Emmaus

On the night of Easter, Jesus, appearing as an ignorant pilgrim, met two Disciples, who were sadly returning to their village, Emmaus. The Disciples, disappointed by Jesus' death, were convinced that their hope that Jesus would be the liberator of Israel had been shattered. They, "foolish" and "slow of heart to believe all that the prophets spoke" (Luke 24:25), didn't understand that, according to the Scriptures, the Messiah would have to suffer to enter into his glory.

The unknown traveler explained these things to the two disappointed Disciples, and they invited him to have supper with them. When he blessed and broke the bread and gave it to them, they recognized him as Jesus, and he immediately disappeared.

The risen Lord celebrated the Eucharist with them: he read and expounded the Word, explaining that all things are summed up in the mystery of his death and resurrection, and, as at the Last Supper, he offered the bread, which is his Body. It is always he who in the Mass leads us into ardent knowledge of the Bible and distributes the bread and wine consecrated into his Body and Blood.

Thomas: "My Lord and my God!"

When Jesus was risen, he appeared on the night of Easter to the Apostles, bringing his gift of peace and the Spirit. Thomas was not present at the supper, so he did not believe that the Apostles had seen the Lord. He wanted to see him and touch him in person. Jesus, who, after eight days, reappeared in the Apostles' midst even though they had locked the doors, satisfied the terms set by Thomas. He invited Thomas to touch the marks of the wounds in his hands and in his open side. "Do not be unbelieving, but believe," urged Jesus, proclaiming, "Blessed are those who have not seen and have believed." And Thomas responded with the wonderful confession "My Lord and my God!" (John 20:27-29). Paradoxically, the story of doubting Thomas is helpful for all of us, giving us the highest and most beautiful invocation to Jesus.

Jesus, the Good Shepherd

The fourth Sunday of Easter is called Good Shepherd Sunday because it is Jesus who, as the Good Shepherd, draws forth and focuses our prayer on this day. He is a unique Shepherd who commits himself to giving his life for his sheep. The Lord Jesus selected and applied that image to himself, an image that God had reserved for himself in the Old Testament. Jesus fulfilled this image in a surprising way, giving his own life to save the lives of the flock. "I am the good shepherd," he proclaims. "A good shepherd lays down his life for the sheep" (John 10:11). Jesus did this by dying on the cross.

Now that he has risen, he guides us personally: he knows us by name and takes care of each one of us. Jesus even looks for us when we are lost. This is why we can say, "The Lord is my shepherd; I shall not want. . . . Even though I walk in the dark valley I fear no evil; for you are at my side" (Ps. 23:1-4).

Peter, Shepherd of the Flock

Before the Risen One ascended to heaven, he entrusted his Disciples to Peter, and asked Peter to love him more than all the others. Peter would represent him and feed — as Jesus calls them — his lambs and his sheep. In fact, Peter does not own them; Christians belong to the Lord. But the Apostle will make the Lord visible, near to them as their Good Shepherd.

From Peter, this mission, which is a grace and a service of love, has passed to his successors, the Bishops of Rome. The Pope is a sure and unfailing sign of Christ's presence in his Church. In his word and in his guidance, we find the very word and guidance of Jesus.

The Ascension

Jesus Rises to Heaven

Forty days after Easter we celebrate Jesus' ascension to heaven. By frequently appearing to his Disciples during those forty days, he had ensured their faith in his resurrection, and he had spoken to them about the reign of God. Now he could return to the Father. But his return was not an abandonment, so we should not be sad. The Ascension is a festive commemoration.

The Ascension of the Lord into heaven gave joy to the Father, who was pleased with the love and obedience of his Son. It also inspired joy in Jesus himself, who by dying and rising had saved humankind, and entered into glory. And the Ascension is a source of joy for us. "In your Son ascended to heaven," we say today in prayer, "our humanity is lifted next to you, O Father, and we, members of his body, live in the hope of being reunited in heaven with our glorious head." The redemption is successful, and all the universe rejoices in the majesty of Jesus, who alone has gone before us into heaven and is waiting for us there.

The Outpouring of the Spirit

At the end of the fiftieth day from the Resurrection, the Lord, glorious at the right hand of the Father, sent the Holy Spirit upon the Disciples. On the Feast of Pentecost, which is as solemn as that of Easter, the liturgy commemorates this outpouring. This is a very great gift of the Father, won by Jesus on the cross.

The Holy Spirit is the life of the Church. From the

Spirit, the source of every grace, the Church
receives the words of Christ and the
wisdom to understand them. By the Spirit,
the body of Christ is consecrated in the Eucharist,
and the other sacraments are made efficacious.

It is the Spirit who, guiding Christians to Jesus,
makes them recognize him and forms him in
their souls. It is also the Spirit who infuses
Christians with wisdom and the light
of counsel. And it is he who gives
force to their preaching.

Pentecost concludes the
Easter Season, and Ordinary
Time begins again.

Trinity Sunday

The Father, the Son, and the Holy Spirit

The Sunday after Pentecost is Trinity Sunday. Of course, the Trinity is always celebrated. The Church's prayer is always addressed to the Father, through his Son, Jesus, in the Holy Spirit. However, on this day, we concentrate with special care on this "Mystery of

Part Three
SOME SOLEMNITIES IN ORDINARY TIME

Faith," which is at the beginning of all and which Jesus revealed to us. In fact, only the Son of God could have spoken to us of the Father and of the Holy Spirit, which unites them in a bond of indescribable love.

When we are in heaven, our inexhaustible joy will consist of contemplating the Trinity, which even now is not far, since it lives in the depths of our hearts by grace.

Corpus Christi

The Body and Blood of the Lord

The Lord's Body is actually celebrated throughout the liturgical year. Every Mass is a memorial of the passion of Jesus, who is truly present on the altar. But the Church has also reserved a special feast to meditate on the miraculous transformation of bread and wine into the Body and Blood of Christ, which is called "transubstantiation." By the power of the very words of the Lord — "This is my body; this is the cup of my blood" — and by the grace of the Holy Spirit, bread and wine are transformed even though they still look the same. They are not a mere symbol or a simple reminder of the presence of Jesus. Christ is truly present in both the bread and the wine.

This is why we venerate Christ present in the Blessed Sacrament. We make visits to the tabernacle, where the Blessed Sacrament is kept after Mass, and pray to Christ present there as a sign of our love. We place the Blessed Sacrament in a monstrance, where we can see Christ present, and we kneel to adore him. We also carry the Blessed Sacrament in solemn procession.

Christic the King

Jesus, Lord of the Universe

The Feast of Christ the King concludes the liturgical year and prefigures what will happen when all the years of earth will have come to an end. History will be finished, and Jesus will appear as the Lord of the universe, the beginning and the end, the one in whom and for whom all has been created.

But the kingship of Jesus is completely different from the kingship of this world. He "has become the Lord, sacrificing himself." His throne was the cross; his weapons are truth, justice, and love. The kingdom of Jesus is now building itself silently and mysteriously in the hearts of believers. Day after day Jesus accompanies them with his grace in order to make them participants in his eternal glory.

The liturgical year is overflowing with the blessings of God and the gifts of Christ the King.

Table of Contents